An opinio

KIDS'
LONDON

Written by
EMMY WATTS

Photography by
MARTIN USBORNE
and DAVID POST

Museum of London (no. 5)

INFORMATION IS DEAD.
LONG LIVE OPINION.

If all information is online, aren't books pointless? (Especially this one.)

Nope. Because what you can't find in the jungle of the internet is concise, expert opinion. Emmy Watts (the brilliant writer) and we (the mediocre publishers) live in this city, love this city, and have young kids who thrive in this city. Whether you are visiting with children or already live here with them, this is our hard-won advice on the absolute best places to go, play and relax. Oh, and the kids will like them too.

Our other opinionated guides:

East London

London Architecture

Vegan London

London Green Spaces

Independent London

London Pubs

Sweet London

This page: Horniman Museum and Gardens (no.25)
Opposite: Dalston Curve Garden (no.24)

King's Cross (no.8)

This page: Biodiversity Playground (no.19)
Opposite: Bob & Blossom (no.18)

LONDON WITH KIDS
(YES, REALLY)

'London is a terrible place for kids!' seems to be the resounding opinion of almost every non-Londoner I've ever met. Ask why, and they'll usually reel off a list of baseless claims that make it sound like we're inhabiting some kind of Dickensian dystopia, forever dodging sooty-faced pickpockets and an outbreak of cholera. And alright, I'll (grudgingly) admit that with its virtually buggy-inaccessible tube network and exasperatingly infrequent baby-change, London might not be the *most* convenient city in which to herd tiny tourists.

But what London lacks in user-friendliness, it makes up for in almost literally everything else. You want parks? It's got 3,000. In fact, nearly half the capital's footprint is made up of green space, meaning a toddler-emancipation opportunity is never far away. And I'm not just talking about a nice patch of grass – we've got some of the most imaginative playscapes on the planet, from Danish playground master Monstrum's pondlife-themed play area in Stratford (no.19) to Regent's Park's coiled concrete dream (no.6).

Kids craving some culture? Prepare them for sensory overload: London is bursting with opportunities to civilise your little urchins, from museums designed to make virtually every subject under the sun accessible to infants, to never-ending, family-friendly art in the form of urban trails, interactive installations and gallery-run kids' sessions.

And it's not all about the kids, either. In fact, it's never been easier for us to reclaim some semblance of our preparental selves – whether that's picking up something that's just for us at one of the capital's stylish family stores or grabbing a genuinely good cup of coffee at a brilliant play café. Thanks to the countless local businesses who've deduced that parents crave enjoyable experiences too, we need never slurp from a polystyrene cup in a sad soft play again.

The absolute best thing about this sprawling great metropolis though, is *choice*. Endless, inexhaustible choice. I mean, where else can your kids play in a 1970s duplex caravan that's been decked out as a stately home (Sutton House and Breaker's Yard, no.15)? Or ride a cable car to – basically – nowhere (Emirates Air Line, no.33)? And how many cities can boast a bookshop dedicated to representing every single child who lives there (Round Table Books, no.32)? With infinite opportunities to gain new experiences, expand their imaginations and simply be the most authentic versions of themselves, London kids are some of the luckiest on Earth.

But I don't need to tell you any of this, really. If you needed convincing that London is a great place for kids, then you probably wouldn't have picked up this book. You just want to know, of the million-and-one places you could drag them to, which are the out-and-out best. Well, here they are.

Emmy Watts
London, June 2021

THE BEST FOR...

Meeting non-parent friends
Seeking a kid-friendly hangout with a grown-up edge? Peckham Levels' (no.27) crowd-pleasing highlights include art, bars and a colourful play area, while Dalston Curve Garden's (no.24) winning mix of beer, pizza and ride-on toys offers excitement for all ages.

A child-friendly lunch
Good food is seldom enough to occupy little ones when it comes to eating out, as most parents are painfully aware. Toconoco (no.48), The Holly Tree (no.21) and PICNIC (no.36) all offer delicious grub in attractive surroundings with a substantial side order of fun that'll keep even the squirmiest tots occupied.

Long hot days
There's only one thing to do with sticky children on a scorching day, and that's install them in the nearest play fountain. Top sprinkler spots include Queen Elizabeth Olympic Park (no.17), King's Cross (no.8) and the Southbank Centre (no.30), while Victoria Park (no.10) has gone one better with its own splash pool.

Grand days out
An all-day excursion with preschoolers? You've got to be kidding. Then again, when ZSL London Zoo (no.7), The Magic Garden at Hampton Court Palace (no.35) and The Children's Garden at Kew (no.42) are all so reassuringly childproof, it would be rude not to.

Playgrounds

Little Londoners are spoilt for choice when it comes to imaginative playgrounds, but special mentions go to Holland Park's wooden wonderland (no.39), Regent's Park's vision in concrete (no.6), Paddington Recreation Ground's themed playscape (no.44) and Queen Elizabeth Olympic Park's breathtakingly beautiful Tumbling Bay (no.17).

Rainy afternoons

The capital's regular rain showers don't have to stop you leaving the house thanks to indoor heroes Discover Children's Story Centre (no.13) and Museum of London Docklands (no.14), which both offer a café, play area and the feeling that your welcome will never be outstayed.

Cute gifts

The quality (and quantity) of London's independent children's stores makes shopping small easy. Try Molly Meg (no.47) for dreamy accessories, Round Table Books (no.32) for inclusive picture books, Bob & Blossom (no.18) for birthday number tees, Cissy Wears (no.9) for something extra special, and Niddle Noddle (no.50) for literally everything else.

Culture with kids

London is packed with inspiring spaces to fire young imaginations. Budding Jackson Pollocks should head to Tate Modern (no.29), while little historians can get hands-on at London Transport Museum (no.1), National Army Museum (no.41) and The Postal Museum's (no.3) dedicated children's galleries.

1

LONDON TRANSPORT MUSEUM

Hands-on history of urban transportation

A fascination with 'things that go' is not a prerequisite for a successful trip to this popular museum. It's relatively compact, but its clever design and engaging interactives still make for a grand day out, whatever your kids are into. Boarding the vintage vehicles is obligatory, while following the Stamper Trail will ensure you don't miss a thing. But it's the two-storey 'play zone' – complete with double-decker, soft-play tube train and 'Thames Nipper' – that'll really jump-start their imaginations.

Covent Garden Piazza, WC2E 7BB
Nearest station: Covent Garden
Paid entry for adults; kids go free
ltmuseum.co.uk

2

CORAM'S FIELDS

Children's-only park with poignant history

Old-London magic abounds at this seven-acre Bloomsbury park, which was built on the site of Thomas Coram's Foundling Hospital. Nearly four centuries later it's still devoted to children, with access granted only to adults in possession of one. Admittedly it's at its best in the summer months, when its abundant trees and sandy water-play area provide welcome respite from the city heat, but it remains a perennial hit thanks to its central location, daily under-5s drop-in and varied play equipment. Make time for a visit to the neighbouring Foundling Museum, a family-geared institution dedicated to telling the moving history of the site.

93 Guilford Street, WC1N 1DN
Nearest station: Russell Square
coramsfields.org

3

THE POSTAL MUSEUM

A day out to write home about

If only all excursions with kids could be as perfect as a trip to The Postal Museum. Just big enough to fill a day and just small enough to be manageable, this relative newbie packs a brilliantly toddler-friendly punch with its family-geared café, underground Mail Rail ride and endless interactives – including a pneumatic tube that will see their message whizzed across the museum, and the chance to star on a postage stamp. The best bit? A themed play space with its own mail-sorting system and pint-sized post office. First class.

15–20 Phoenix Place, WC1X 0DA
Nearest station: Farringdon
Paid entry
postalmuseum.org

4

BARBICAN CENTRE

Family fun in an enigmatic arts hub

Brutalism and babies: not an obvious match, but one that's perfectly made at the Barbican, the iconic arts hub whose hard concrete shell conceals one heck of a family-friendly filling. The sell-out Saturday film club, much-loved children's library and well-conceived family festivals are all good places to start with little ones, but there's just as much fun to be had scooting the endless high walks, racing up and down the labyrinthine staircases or hide-and-seeking among the Conservatory's tropical plants. Savvy parents will vouch for the brilliance of the erstwhile under-5s sessions – keep an eye out for future offerings.

Silk Street, EC2Y 8DS
Nearest station: Barbican
Paid entry to some events and exhibitions
barbican.org.uk

5

MUSEUM OF LONDON

Stirring stories from the city's past

Where better to start with little Londoners than at this institution devoted to the history of their very city? While the capital's eponymous museum has its flaws – most glaringly its obscure location and convoluted one-way system to rival IKEA's – it remains a hit haunt for preschoolers. Interactive highlights include a dynamic London Underground model, a full-scale Saxon house reconstruction and a 1950s-themed early-years gallery. Plus, plans for the museum's move to a colossal site at West Smithfield in 2024 look positively epic.

150 London Wall, EC2Y 5HN
Nearest station: Barbican
museumoflondon.org.uk

6

REGENT'S PARK

Effortless family fun in elegant parkland

You'd have to do something fairly drastic to pull off a bad day in Regent's Park. With its plentiful cafés, 400 acres of strolling space, four massive playgrounds and resident zoo (no.7), it's central London's gift to parents and easily its most painless family outing. Head to the new Gloucester Gate Playground for accessible play in a lush, landscaped utopia, or check out Marylebone Green Playground – a Soviet-chic concrete vision inspired by the park's annual Frieze Sculpture display.

Regent's Park, NW1 4NR
Nearest station: Regent's Park
royalparks.org.uk/parks/the-regents-park

7

ZSL LONDON ZOO

200-year-old inner-city menagerie

There are more than 20,000 creatures to discover at the Zoological Society of London's Regent's Park outpost, and its inanimate attractions warrant a mention too. Take, for example, the Land of the Lions, where an elaborate reconstruction of a Gujarati village all but eclipses the big cats themselves; or the freshly remodelled and ever popular playground with its life-sized hot-air balloon and summertime Splash Zone. Should your kids fancy glimpsing some actual animals, the Penguin Beach, Reptile House and Animal Adventure Zone are all fairly reliable bets.

Outer Circle, Regent's Park, NW1 4RY
Nearest station: Camden Town
Paid entry
zsl.org/zsl-london-zoo

8

KING'S CROSS

Vibrant neighbourhood with plenty for families

Historically, the area north of King's Cross station would be the last place you'd think to take young children. These days, it's worthy of a family day out thanks to a three-million-pound redevelopment that has transformed it from post-industrial no man's land to trendy – but still friendly – urban hub, boasting 67 acres of pedestrianised (aka scooting) space. Reasons to bring the kids here are many, but the unpredictable Granary Square fountains, open-ended PlayKX activity sessions and countless child-friendly restaurants are high on the list. Interactive art installations, family toilets and plentiful coffee shops for parental refuelling help, too.

King's Cross, N1C
Nearest station: King's Cross St. Pancras
kingscross.co.uk

9

CISSY WEARS

Elegant boutique with an ethical focus

Imagine the worst kind of gaudy, plastic-filled juvenile hell... then picture the polar opposite – and that's Cissy Wears. Beginning life as a south London start-up, this concept store might have made its name flogging bibs and bootees, but the vibe is anything but cutesy. Instead, owner Nicola Eyre has created a dreamy masterclass in considered children's wares: from infinitely hand-downable rompers in honeyed shades of milk and caramel to ethnically diverse dolls moulded from vanilla-scented vinyl. It also has of the best children's-book edits we've ever had the pleasure of perusing.

89 Coal Drops Yard, N1C 4DQ
Nearest station: King's Cross St. Pancras
cissywears.com

10

VICTORIA PARK

Perennial fun in over 200 acres of greenery

Two words: splash pool. Vicky Park's gushing maze of snaking concrete canals might be relatively modest size-wise, but it's still one of east London's kid-friendly high points in the summer months, along with the park's armada of blue rowing boats and pedalos. But this sprawling green space isn't a fair-weather wonder. Head here year-round to scale lofty treehouses, zoom down massive slides, spot ducks bobbing on the sparkling lakes and commandeer one of the bountiful follies before refuelling at chilled-out, mum-run café The Hub.

Grove Road, E3 5TB
Nearest station: Cambridge Heath
towerhamlets.gov.uk/victoriapark

11

LUNA & CURIOUS

Lifestyle store with a chic kids' department

In 2017, more than a decade after it set up shop on Tower Hamlets' historic Boundary Estate, self-styled 'miniature department store' Luna & Curious spawned a stylish progeny. Like its parent next door, this small but perfectly formed children's branch focuses on good quality, British-made garments with boundless wearability, as well as sustainable toys selected for their imaginative-play potential. Don't get too jealous though – the grown-up end is just as dreamy. In fact, Luna & Curious stocks several of its childrenswear brands in adult sizes, so you can finally stop lusting after your 5-year-old's threads.

24–26 Calvert Avenue, Shoreditch, E2 7JP
Nearest station: Shoreditch High Street
lunaandcurious.com

12

A SMALL TRIANGLE

Considered design for little ones

This kids' offshoot of independent lifestyle shop
Triangle Store popped up a few doors down from
its parent in early 2020 – to the joy of the well-
dressed and child-laden of Lower Clapton. The
clothes here might be dinkier (products cater to
babies and toddlers), but the vibe is the same: a
pleasing contradiction of tranquillity and playful-
ness, beauty and practicality. Kids are free to poke
around, and the owners are so easy to talk to you
almost find yourself asking for a cuppa. The down-
side? Everything is so ludicrously covetable you'll
half consider burning the contents of your nursery
and starting all over again.

5 Chatsworth Road, E5 0LH
Nearest station: Homerton
trianglestore.co.uk

13

DISCOVER CHILDREN'S STORY CENTRE

Creative play space with immersive exhibitions

A magical woodland. A Bavarian castle. A steampunk flying machine. The connection? Admittedly not much, except that they can all be found inside Discover, Stratford's popular children's literary museum-meets-play centre. Arranged across three floors and a sizeable garden, the space is deliberately ambiguous, with interactive sets designed to inspire imaginative, open-ended play. Highlights include the annual(ish) temporary exhibition – which invites kids to immerse themselves in the world of a particular author or illustrator – and engaging daily story-time sessions.

383–387 High Street, E15 4QZ
Nearest station: Stratford High Street
Paid entry; under-1s go free
discover.org.uk

14

MUSEUM OF LONDON DOCKLANDS

Toddler-geared fun in a historic warehouse

An inspiring play area and a high interactives-to-information ratio make Museum of London's Isle of Dogs outpost just as worthy of a day out as its better-known big sister (no.5). Yet despite its virtues, it's woefully underrated, and a stroll through its exhibits is often a strangely serene affair. Its dedicated children's gallery, Mudlarks, is easily one of London's best, offering docks-themed soft play, copious cargo-loading opportunities and an ever popular water-play table – although sessions are infuriatingly short. Soften the blow with a post-play brownie from the adjoining café.

No. 1 Warehouse, West India Quay, E14 4AL
Nearest station: West India Quay
museumoflondon.org.uk/docklands

15

SUTTON HOUSE AND BREAKER'S YARD

Eccentric museum in the heart of Hackney

The words '500-year-old former squat' don't exactly scream family day out, but – if you're willing to overlook its abundant staircases and the fact that it's almost definitely haunted – the National Trust's only Hackney property makes for a genuinely delightful visit. Young historians are invited to rummage through the toy chests for Tudor puppets and period costumes, or to explore the fully immersive squatters' room with its striking mural and nostalgic chintz. But the real fun starts in the Breaker's Yard – a quirky community garden housing a sandpit and interactive caravan art installation, among other oddities.

2 and 4, Homerton High Street, E9 6JQ
Nearest station: Hackney Central
Paid entry
nationaltrust.org.uk/sutton-house-and-breakers-yard

16

WORD

Chic family lifestyle store

As the saying goes, it takes a village to raise a child – and if by 'raising', you mean kitting them out with killer threads and sustainable accessories, then Walthamstow Village isn't a bad place to start. Conceived in 2016 by then-new mum Anah Parker-Dean, this achingly cool boutique focuses on parent-owned brands, stocking everything from pregnancy teas to leopard-print wallpaper for your toddler's bedroom. Their website is great, but the bricks-and-mortar is better. Head down for post-natal yoga sessions held in store and a visit to Smith & Goat – a plant-and-concrete emporium that's taken up residency in Word's back room.

36 Orford Road, E17 9NJ
Nearest station: Walthamstow Central
Paid tickets for yoga sessions
wordstoreldn.com

17

QUEEN ELIZABETH OLYMPIC PARK

Fountains and frolics in one of London's newest parks

If they were handing out medals for London's best playscapes, Tumbling Bay might just get the gold. Unveiled in 2014, the Olympic Park's award-winning kids' wonderland rejects traditional play equipment in favour of an ambitious design blending swirling rock pools, wobbly bridges, lofty treehouses and endless sand. But the fun doesn't stop there. Head south on balmier days and attempt to outwit the Pleasure Gardens' computer-controlled maze of water jets, or toddle down to nearby East Village for befuddling fun in the Mirror Labyrinth created by Danish artist Jeppe Hein.

Westfield Avenue, E15 2DU
Nearest station: Stratford
queenelizabetholympicpark.co.uk

18

BOB & BLOSSOM

Slogan tees and tutus behind the flower stalls

Columbia Road's invariably heaving Sunday flower market may sound like hell on earth with kids in tow, but once you've elbowed your way through the crowd (or employed the buggy as a battering ram), the street's resident children's boutique offers refuge with its old-world vibes and calming pastel hues. Browse cute picture books and traditional toy cars before inevitably settling on an own-brand birthday tee or fluffy tutu. Alternatively, you could avoid the flower fight and come back another day (it opens Friday to Sunday), but where's the fun in that?

140 Columbia Road, E2 7RG
Nearest station: Hoxton
bobandblossom.co.uk

19

BIODIVERSITY PLAYGROUND

Danish-designed, pondlife-themed play area

A sad wedge of land straddled by a train station, a shopping mall and the ugliest multistorey car park in existence might seem like a poor choice of location for Danish playground master Monstrum's only UK site, but boy will you appreciate it after a harrowing trip to Westfield with the kids. So-called because it's themed around a pond and its inhabitants, the Biodiversity Playground more than makes up for its surroundings with bouncy pink lily pads, origami play boats, bridges to nowhere and a giant, orange koi-fish slide, all lovingly crafted from sustainable timber.

Westfield Stratford City, Montfichet Road, E20 1EJ
Nearest station: Stratford
uk.westfield.com/stratfordcity/kids

20

ROLE2PLAY

Town-themed play centre with a café

Few things sound less relaxing than an entire town run by two-year-olds. Surprisingly, this *Biggleton*-esque play hub is actually one of London's more peaceful toddler hangouts – mostly because they'll be so overwhelmed by activities you won't have to do anything. Potential preschool careers include serving customers at the village coffee shop, working the checkouts at the well-stocked supermarket and constructing foam-brick walls on the local building site. Providing their charge doesn't require an intern, adults can grab a latte in the adjacent café and watch as the chaos unfolds.

75 Fulbourne Road, E17 4EZ
Nearest station: Wood Street
Paid entry for kids; adults and under-1s go free
role2play.com

21

THE HOLLY TREE

East End boozer featuring a miniature railway

There are child-friendly pubs, and then there are pubs with electric trains in their beer gardens. Fully restored in 2019, this smart-but-welcoming watering hole boasts moody views over Wanstead Flats, a decent range of beers and a tempting gastro menu headlined by particularly good fish and chips. One train ticket buys you three surprisingly speedy laps of the outside space: enough of a draw to ensure a steady stream of families. Meanwhile, the adults-only section stops it from becoming a glorified crèche – and makes this a serious date-night candidate.

141 Dames Road, E7 0DZ
Nearest station: Wanstead Park
Paid ticket for miniature railway
thehollytreepub.co.uk

22

WONDROUS THEATRE

Playful family fashion

With a range of clothes so striking they could be stage costumes, Wondrous Theatre more than lives up to its moniker. In-store props in the form of a vintage rocking horse, red racing car and Dutch dolls' house may even grant you a quiet browse of the small but flawless collection, which comprises both local and international women's and kids' labels. Bold colours and clever cuts stand out, but the quality of the fabric steals this delightfully eccentric show, and caressing everything in sight feels inevitable.

60 Dalston Lane, E8 3AH
Nearest station: Dalston Junction
wondroustheatre.com

23

MOTHERS HUB

Family store with a community focus

An unassuming façade and underrated location belie this cosy store's brilliance. A long-time lynchpin of Walthamstow's under-10s scene, this Wood Street wonder does exactly what its name promises: provides E17ers not just with a place to kit out their kids with cool clothes, but with a neighbourhood nucleus offering in-store classes, a pre-loved exchange scheme and lush self-care products. Local labels are championed, and you can even pick up an in-house exclusive from co-owner Suzie Smith's gorgeously sustainable range.

133 Wood Street, E17 3LX
Nearest station: Wood Street
mothershub.co.uk

24

DALSTON CURVE GARDEN

Urban oasis with a café and communal toys

An assortment of aggressively pre-loved ride-ons, the highlighter-bright, geometrically patterned stage and a programme of toddler-friendly events ensure this neighbourhood garden's popularity with little ones, while a café serving locally sourced booze – enjoyed in moderation, one would hope – makes it a hit with their grown-ups. It looks its best in the summer months, but is worth a visit all year round thanks to a ready supply of blankets, homemade soup and mulled drinks. Head here in October for the annual Pumpkin Lantern Festival, where 1,000 glinting eyes are a spooky sight to behold.

13 Dalston Lane, E8 3DF
Nearest station: Dalston Junction
dalstongarden.org

25

HORNIMAN MUSEUM AND GARDENS

Family-centric museum in scenic grounds

Where to start with the Horniman? You could head to its Natural History Gallery, where top-notch taxidermy is arranged in crawler-friendly cabinets. Or try Nature Base, the hands-on children's learning centre. What about the interactive Music Gallery, where kids are free to make a magnificent racket? Or one of the consistently great temporary exhibitions. Want live animals? Under-3s go free at the aquarium, and at the Animal Walk resident goats, rabbits and alpacas wait primed for the petting. Add rambling gardens, a delightful café and considered family facilities, and you're looking at one of south London's most wholesome days out.

100 London Road, SE23 3PQ
Nearest station: Forest Hill
Paid entry to some attractions
horniman.ac.uk

Please do not
touch the walrus
or sit on the iceberg

26

BATTERSEA PARK

Wholesome Thameside green space

There's barely an inch of Battersea Park's 200 acres that isn't geared towards families, from its pedalo-strewn boating lake to its frankly preposterous quantity of ice-cream kiosks. On its own this Victorian gem is a spectacular setting for a lazy family picnic, an after-school kickabout and maybe one of the best games of hide-and-seek you'll ever play – and that's before you've considered its extracurricular offerings. Head to the impressive main playground with its looming Go Ape high ropes, or visit the perfectly proportioned Children's Zoo – a grand day out in its own right.

Albert Bridge Road, SW11 4NJ
Nearest station: Battersea Park
Paid entry to some attractions
batterseapark.org

27

PECKHAM LEVELS

Hip cultural hub with lots to explore

Why drag your kids to a multi-storey carpark in Peckham? Well, to be fair, only the bottom level is a carpark these days. The other six have been transformed into a creative hub hosting a co-working space, street-food outlets and trendy bars. Not the most obvious family hangout, but its halfpipe-like play area, interactive art and famous rainbow stairs offer endless glee for infants, while the cafés and roomy toilets (bring your own changing mat) mean you can settle in for the day. Looking to, ahem, level up your experience? Try Plonk's nine-hole golf or Family Yoga at LEVELSIX studios.

95a Rye Lane, SE15 4ST
Nearest station: Peckham Rye
Paid entry to some events and attractions
peckhamlevels.org

28

NATIONAL MARITIME MUSEUM

Seafaring adventures for families

Whether your little one's a would-be buccaneer or a timorous landlubber, a trip to the capital's only sea-themed museum is always a good idea thanks to its brilliant family facilities, plentiful themed galleries and emphasis on interactivity. Mini mariners are invited to take on a variety of nautical tasks across the museum's three main hands-on areas, including firing cannons at pesky pirate vessels, leading a fleet of model ships across a huge interactive atlas, commandeering a replica of a historical merchant cruiser, or just donning a stripy apron and becoming a juvenile fishmonger. Whatever floats their boat, basically.

Romney Road, SE10 9NF
Nearest station: Cutty Sark
Paid entry to some exhibits
rmg.co.uk

29

TATE MODERN

Contemporary gallery offering family activities

Tate may have missed a trick by failing to accommodate a permanent kids' area within its gargantuan halls, but you'll still find plenty to occupy little ones here. The family events and experimental Tate Exchange workshops are worth dropping in on, while a wander through the permanent galleries should inspire even the most cynical of mini art critics. Staff are pretty hawk-eyed where kids are concerned, and some exhibitions are more family friendly than others, but the vast Turbine Hall with its thought-provoking annual commission is always a winner. The shop's brilliant children's offering demands a look, too.

Bankside, SE1 9TG
Nearest station: Blackfriars
Paid entry to some exhibits
tate.org.uk

30

SOUTHBANK CENTRE

*Welcoming cultural hub with a vibrant
kids' programme*

In search of an easy day out? This sprawling arts complex is a haven for young families with its abundant amenities, ample seating, packed events schedule and – wait for it – singing lift. Regular 'Rug Rhymes' and preschool gamelan sessions pull in the baby and toddler crowd, while seemingly endless staircases mean they'll probably never want to leave. Outside, artist Jeppe Hein's mischievous fountain is a welcome summer distraction, and the colourfully graffitied Skate Space is a top spot for ollie-watching. Head here in February for the annual Imagine Children's Festival – a half-term must.

Belvedere Road, SE1 8XX
Nearest station: Waterloo
Paid entry to some events and exhibits
southbankcentre.co.uk

31

GENTLY ELEPHANT

More than just a shoe shop

Wall-to-wall shelves heaving with expertly curated games and craft kits take up one half of this roomy Brockley boutique. The other is all anatomically correct dolls, new-collection Mini Rodini (no.37) and cute pocket-money toys. It might identify as a shoe shop, but Gently Elephant's unconventional layout can make footwear feel like an afterthought: a heap of jellies in a basket, boxes of Hummel trainers piled high by the till. Don't be fooled though, you'll still find just what you're after, be it seaside-ready Salt-Water sandals or school-approved Mary Janes – or yes, even Crocs.

169 Brockley Road, SE4 2RS
Nearest station: Brockley
Other locations: Crofton Park, Ladywell, Harefield
gentlyelephant.co.uk

32

ROUND TABLE BOOKS

Inclusive children's bookstore

The fairy lights that surround this tiny store's signage are the first clue that you've stumbled across something rather magical. The second is that every single book it sells is an underrepresented tale, be it a disability-themed picture book or an anti-racist manifesto for teens (something that really shouldn't be out of the ordinary, but is). The best part though is the way every book is a celebration – and not just an acknowledgement – of diversity, and that each child who enters can leave with a new literary hero who truly represents them.

97 Granville Arcade, Coldharbour Lane, sw9 8ps
Nearest station: Brixton
roundtablebooks.co.uk

Little Leaders

BOLD WOMEN
IN
BLACK HISTORY

VASHTI HARRISON

33

EMIRATES AIR LINE

Cross-Thames cable-car voyage

It might not take you anywhere useful and the contrived air-travel vocabulary is fairly annoying, but that doesn't stop this souped-up ski lift from being a pretty dependable hit with young kids. A one-way trip only takes five minutes, although if you're boarding at North Greenwich then you might as well cough up for the return trip since there's little to nothing to see in Royal Docks (unless your offspring are particularly keen to visit the ExCeL Centre). Choose a windy day for added thrills.

Units 1–4, Edmund Halley Way, SE10 0FR
Nearest station: North Greenwich
Other terminal: Royal Docks
Paid ticket
emiratesairline.co.uk

34

APPLE TREE CHILDREN'S CAFÉ

Parkside play café aimed at under-5s

It might call itself a children's café, but Apple Tree's genius lies in its ability to tap into what adults crave most. We're talking good coffee (from Brixton-based Volcano Coffee Works), plenty to occupy the kids (there's a new role-play activity every week), and – most crucially – an almost complete absence of gaudy plastic crap. Emily Ajasa took over what was a tired soft-play-and-a-cuppa situation opposite Brockwell Park in 2018, and transformed it into this stylish spot – now one of south London's most popular parental destinations.

27–29 Norwood Road, SE24 9AA
Nearest station: Herne Hill
Paid tickets for play sessions
appletreelondon.com

35

THE MAGIC GARDEN AT HAMPTON COURT PALACE

Inspiring play area in Tudor palace grounds

So what if it's a 21st-century addition to a 16th-century palace? With its inventive design, full acre of recreation space and self-contained café, this fantasy-themed playground is a day out in its own right. Traditional equipment has been shunned in favour of towering castles and a ruby-eyed dragon to clamber on, and the result is a richer, more imaginative play experience. Undulating hills give way to swirling slides and jaunty tepees, while hidden pathways reveal mythical beasts and secret dens. What's more, a ticket to the Magic Garden includes entry to Hampton Court's famous 300-year-old maze, just next door.

Hampton Court Palace, Hampton Court Way, KT8 9AU
Nearest station: Hampton Court
Paid entry
hrp.org.uk/hampton-court-palace

36

PICNIC

Stylish role-play centre with a café

Childhood is filled with indisputable truths: puddles are for jumping in, farts are hysterical, and playing at being a grown-up is the most fun you can have without sugar. Fortunately, pretending to have responsibilities has never been easier thanks to London's recent surge in Toytown-style role-play centres, and this smart Kingston hangout tops the charts. Its upscale play street features a theatre, police station and even an NHS health centre, as well as an impressive café offering kids' portions of everything. Safety gates, ultra-clean facilities and a handy baby-plonking area up the convenience factor, making a visit here... well, a picnic.

Unit 3, Rotunda Centre, Clarence Street, KT1 1QJ
Nearest station: Kingston
Paid entry; babies under 6 months go free
picnicandplay.co.uk

37

MINI RODINI

Sustainable kidswear in quirky, covetable prints

This illustrator-founded brand only has one shop outside of its native Sweden, making the Notting Hill branch practically a religious pilgrimage for its fans. For the uninitiated, expect kitschy, conversational prints depicting everything from stony-eyed mermen to a coquettish Princess Di. Though several London stores carry Mini Rodini ranges, only this standalone can offer the full immersive experience. Murals of their best-known characters cover the walls, there's almost always a freebie and the aptly named Treasures Room is full of repaired and reworked past-season gems.

237 Westbourne Grove, W11 2SE
Nearest station: Notting Hill Gate
minirodini.com

38

DIANA MEMORIAL PLAYGROUND

Vast wooden playscape inspired by Peter Pan

Plenty of playgrounds have pirate ships, but you'll be hard-pushed to find one as impressive as the Diana Memorial's centrepiece – a fully rigged Jolly Roger sailing a sea of sand. Opened in 2000 in tribute to the late Princess of Wales, this enchanting space enjoys enduring popularity thanks to an inclusive design, a reassuring 'no unaccompanied adults' policy, and an impalpable magic that'll make you wish you'd never grown up. Round off summer visits with a trip to the nearby play fountain, a cascading loop of splashy joy.

Kensington Gardens, Broad Walk, W2 4RU
Nearest station: Queensway
royalparks.org.uk

39

HOLLAND PARK

54 acres of family-friendly green space

Affable peacocks. Baby changing in the men's toilets. The unlikely but very real possibility of befriending celebrity parents. There were already myriad reasons to take the kids to this leafy corner of Kensington, even before the adventure playground got a spectacular one-million-pound upgrade. These days, a family visit will likely be dominated by this handsome new addition, though its soaring structures mean the sandy toddler playground is still a better bet for tinies. End warmer days with a visit to the Design Museum's forecourt play fountain – handily located within splashing distance.

Ilchester Place, W8 6LU
Nearest station: Holland Park
rbkc.gov.uk

40

THE CONRAN SHOP

Design-led toys and kids' furniture

Tangerine walls, accommodating staff and numerous 'invitations for play' make for a fun and stress-free browse around the Conran kids' section, even with a tornado of a toddler in tow. The selection here is predictably flawless, with products ranging from well-chosen pocket-money toys to stuff-of-dreams treehouse beds. It's pricy but that doesn't mean you can't try before you buy; children are actively encouraged to take advantage of the ride-on-ready trikes and tiny ping-pong tables. Only the perilous proximity to the ceramics department stops you from relaxing entirely.

81 Fulham Road, SW3 6RD
Nearest station: South Kensington
Other locations: Marylebone, Selfridges
conranshop.com

41

NATIONAL ARMY MUSEUM

Military museum with exceptional soft play

Does your toddler fancy themselves as the next G.I. Jane? Great. Or have no interest in the military whatsoever? That's fine too. In fact, NAM's recent multi-million-pound redevelopment has rendered it so family friendly it could be a museum of virtually anything and still be a guaranteed parental victory. The galleries are sprawling but easy to navigate, with ample interactives to occupy tiny hands. State-of-the-art facilities and a spacious café serving free kids' meals are both big draws, but it's the museum's incredible barracks-themed play space that will guarantee your frequent return.

Royal Hospital Road, sw3 4ht
Nearest station: Sloane Square
Paid entry to some attractions
nam.ac.uk

42

THE CHILDREN'S GARDEN AT KEW

Inventive play space in a botanical garden

Designed to foster a passion for nature in all who play there, Kew Garden's inspiring space for 2–12-year-olds is themed around the things that plants need to grow. High points include the sandpit-submerged Earth Garden with its tubular 'wormhole' slides, the Air Garden's vibrant 'pollen' spheres, and the imposing aerial walkway at the garden's core. It's so brilliant, you'll want to stay all day. Sadly, sessions are limited to 90 minutes.

Royal Botanic Gardens, Kew, TW9 3AE
Nearest station: Kew Gardens
Paid entry to Royal Botanic Gardens
kew.org

43

SCIENCE MUSEUM

Inspiring, extra interactive exhibits

You might think you know the Science Museum, but this South Kensington classic can be overwhelming with young kids if you don't have a fixed itinerary. Start with a bang in the impressive Space exhibit, then stop off at the multi-sensory Pattern Pod to test their symmetry skills and the 'Who Am I?' gallery for some genealogical fun. Next, make your way to The Garden, a small but well-loved basement play area that's great for 1–6s (despite its recommended 3–6s age bracket). Wonderlab costs extra and is technically aimed at older kids, but don't let that stop you – it's got really cool slides.

Exhibition Road, SW7 2DD
Nearest station: South Kensington
Paid entry to some exhibits
sciencemuseum.org.uk

44

PADDINGTON RECREATION GROUND

Impressive playground in a Victorian park

In darkest Maida Vale you'll find a very rare sort of playground – one inspired by Paddington Bear. As themes go it's subtle but look closely and you'll find numerous nods: there's the wonky steam liner primed for ursine stowaways; a row of pastel playhouses resembling the Brown family's Notting Hill street; and even a scaled-down recreation of Paddington Station. All ages are catered for and even adults get a good deal in the form of unusually good coffee from the park café, which also serves pizza and ice cream. No marmalade sandwiches though, sadly.

Randolph Avenue, w9 1pd
Nearest station: Maida Vale
everyoneactive.com/centre/paddington-recreation-ground

45

WHAT MOTHER MADE

Heirloom-worthy kidswear

Sure, the clothes are vintage-inspired and the name conjures visions of *Andy Pandy*, but there's nothing passé about this impossibly chic family boutique with its planet-friendly practices and cool, contemporary vibe. Whether you're in the market for a jazzy kids' romper or a breastfeeding-friendly smock dress, you'll find it here – and literally nowhere else, thanks to an in-house team who'll custom-sew whatever your heart desires in their Hackney workshop. 'Mother', aka founder Charlotte Denn, offers an immaculate toy and book edit alongside her dreamy garments, but she's not precious when it comes to little hands testing the stock. In fact, it's encouraged.

166 Stoke Newington Church Street, N16 0JL
Nearest station: Stoke Newington
Other location: Homerton
whatmothermade.co.uk

46

RAF MUSEUM

Flight-themed fun

Aerial warfare isn't everyone's cup of tea, but the museum formerly known as Hendon Aerodrome isn't half as niche as you'd expect. Head down there on a weekday morning and the only aviation enthusiasts you'll find will be a bunch of plane-spotting preschoolers earning their stripes at the weekly under-5s sessions or climbing aboard the abundant model aircraft. Aspiring pilots will love exploring the historic hangars, which house more than 100 notable aircraft, and even mini aviophobes will be flying high when they see the themed playground – one of the capital's most imaginative.

Grahame Park Way, NW9 5LL
Nearest station: Colindale
rafmuseum.org.uk

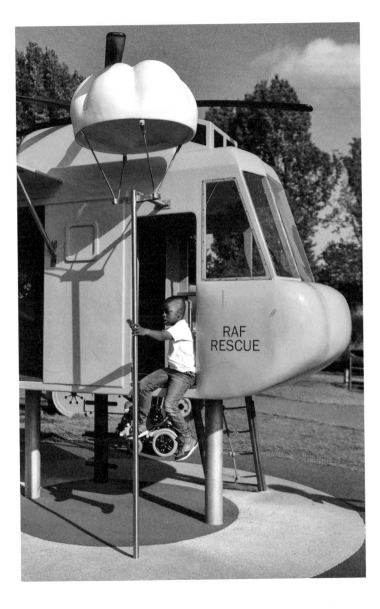

47

MOLLY MEG

Interior design for modern kids

This Essex Road indie is so tightly packed with
treasures it can be hard to get your buggy through
the door, but persevere and you're in for a tasteful
treat. Expertly curated by ex-kidswear designer
Molly Price, this is your one-stop shop for ridicu-
lously cool nursery furniture, design-led baby gifts,
aesthetically pleasing party supplies and handmade
fancy-dress costumes, among many other delights.
The shop's occasional in-store art workshops are
a reliable sell-out, and with good reason – follow
them on Instagram to be the first to sign up.

111 Essex Road, N1 2SL
Nearest station: Essex Road
mollymeg.com

48

TOCONOCO

Unpretentious Japanese play café

A concealed location and unmarked façade might have spelt disaster for a lesser establishment, but this canal-side café boasts a loyal clientele made up of both child-laden and child-free locals. Its name, which translates as 'kids on the floor', should be taken literally, meaning it can be a touch chaotic – especially in the back room that houses its built-in play corner – but that's all part of the charm. Simple noodle soups and rice balls go down well with kids, and you can't visit without trying a matcha blondie and black sesame latte.

Unit A, 28 Hertford Road, N1 5QT
Nearest station: Haggerston
toconoco.com

49

BEAR + WOLF

Stylish café with a sizeable playroom

Laptop-wielding freelancers and rowdy toddlers unite at this crowd-pleasing Tufnell Park café, which manages to retain an air of cool despite the often-overwhelming presence of the latter. Sure, it's unusually family friendly with its hook-on high-chairs, always-overflowing buggy park, toy-stuffed 'cubroom' and children's menu, but the contemporary décor and biodynamic Ozone coffee keep the grown-ups just as interested. In summer, the cute courtyard comes into its own. Gather your kids, some toys and a frozen strawberry smoothie, and settle down in the sun. Bliss.

153 Fortess Road, NW5 2HR
Nearest station: Tufnell Park
bearandwolfcafe.com

50

NIDDLE NODDLE

Nostalgic children's store with a modern edge

Kids' shops don't get much more perfect than this, the jewel in Crouch End's famously family-friendly crown. Conceived by Katrine Camillo and Eilidh Fraser as a nod to the toyshops of their youth, Niddle Noddle is an effortless fusion of vintage charm and contemporary design. A focus on durability means some of the stock is on the pricier side, but timeless designs equal endless hand-me-down potential, and a table laden with pocket-money toys keeps things accessible. Still need convincing? The banana-yellow helter-skelter might just do the trick.

5 Topsfield Parade, N8 8PR
Nearest station: Crouch Hill
niddlenoddle.com

INDEX

IMAGE CREDITS

CONTRIBUTORS

Emmy Watts writes about cool things for tiny Londoners on her blog bablands.com and lives in Camden with her two kids, who've both visited all 50 places in this book (many, many times).

Martin Usborne is a photographer, new dad and co-founder of Hoxton Mini Press. There is no link between these facts and him getting the job on the book.

David Post is a Canadian-born, London-based photographer whose images feature on MAST chocolate bars, as well as in several books by Hoxton Mini Press.

Hoxton Mini Press is a small indie publisher making books about London with a dedication to good photography and lovely production. Founders Martin and Ann's two daughters, Olive and Hazel, appear in many of the shots in this guide only through sheer coincidence.

An Opinionated Guide to Kids' London
First edition, second printing

Published in 2021 by Hoxton Mini Press, London
Copyright © Hoxton Mini Press 2021. All rights reserved.

Text by Emmy Watts
Photography by Martin Usborne*
Copy-editing by Florence Filose
Design by Daniele Roa
Production by Anna De Pascale
Production and editorial support by Becca Jones

*Except for photography by David Post and additional images
credited on previous page.

With thanks to Matthew Young for initial series design.

Please note: we recommend checking the websites listed for each
entry before you visit for the latest information on price, opening times
and pre-booking requirements.

A CIP catalogue record for this book is available from the British Library.
The rights of Emmy Watts, Martin Usborne and David Post to be identified
as the creators of this Work have been asserted under the Copyright,
Designs and Patents Act 1988.

ISBN: 978-1-910566-98-5

Printed and bound by OZGraf, Poland

Hoxton Mini Press is an environmentally conscious publisher,
committed to offsetting our carbon footprint. The offset for this book
was purchased from Stand For Trees.

For every book you buy from our website, we plant a tree:
www.hoxtonminipress.com